The Earth Is Good

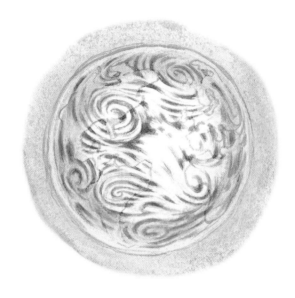

"The plants and animals
know our thoughts."

Gäy onõ seh
Seneca Elder and Clan Mother

The Earth Is Good

A Chant
in Praise of Nature

Michael DeMunn

Illustrated by
Jim McMullan

J
550
DEM

SCHOLASTIC INC.
New York Toronto London Auckland Sydney

To Ellen, Betsy and Carl:
dear friends who love the earth
and who have touched so many lives,
especially mine
—M.D.

For Rob B.
—J.M.

Text copyright © 1999 by Michael DeMunn.
Illustrations copyright © 1999 by Jim McMullan.
All rights reserved. Published by Scholastic Inc.
SCHOLASTIC and its related logos are registered trademarks of Scholastic Inc.

16.00

Library of Congress Cataloging-in-Publication Data

DeMunn, Michael.
The earth is good / by Michael DeMunn; illustrated by Jim McMullan.
p.   cm.
Summary: Simple text and illustrations introduce the earth and its treasures, including its trees, flowers, animals, and weather.
ISBN 0-590-35010-2
[1. Earth—Juvenile literature. [1. Earth.] I. McMullan, Jim, 1936- ill. II. Title.
QB631.4.D4   1999
550—dc21   97-51345   CIP   AC

10   9   8   7   6   5   4   3   2   1   9/9   0/0   01   02   03   04

Printed in Singapore   46
First printing, March 1999

The sun is good.

The earth is good.

The trees

and birds
and bees
are good.
The flowers
are good.

The mouse,
the worm,
the soil
are good.

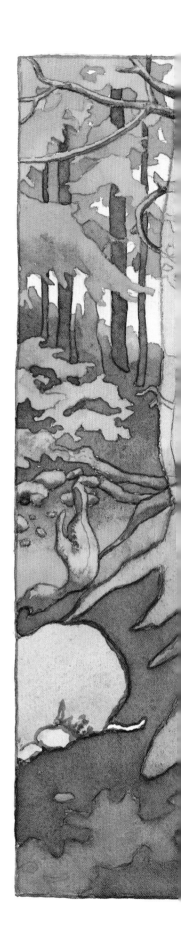

The wind
and rain
are good.

The rivers
are good.

The fish are good.

The oceans

and whales
are good.

The
mountains
are good.

The sun
is good;
the day
is good.

The moon,
the stars,
the night
are good.

The earth
is good.

And you are good.